MAGICIAN
OF THE
BEAUTIFUL

MAGICIAN OF THE BEAUTIFUL

An Introduction to Neville Goddard

Mitch Horowitz
author of *The Miracle Club*

Published 2019 by Gildan Media LLC
aka G&D Media
www.GandDmedia.com

Front cover design by David Rheinhardt of Pyrographx

Interior design by Meghan Day Healey of Story Horse, LLC

Library of Congress Cataloging-in-Publication Data is available
upon request

ISBN: 978-1-7225-0283-6

10   9   8   7   6   5   4   3   2   1

Contents

Author's Note

This short book is adapted from a presentation called "Magician of the Beautiful," which I delivered in New York City in March 2019. In some cases, I paraphrase Neville's statements from his lectures. All other quotations are verbatim. I wish to thank Christine Alfred and Bobby Picciotto for organizing and recording the original event.

LIVING FROM WITHIN

1

For some of you, this may be an introduction to Neville. For me, it's an opportunity to talk about the ideas of a figure who has been life-changing. For the past fifteen years or so, among all the various metaphysical systems that I study, work with, and write about, Neville has been my primary influence.

Nevertheless, I don't venerate spiritual figures or writers to the point where I think they cannot be questioned, improved upon, or understood to have been wrong about certain things. However much I love these figures, however much their lives and ideas have meant to me, I also find that we as human beings seem to possess an almost instinctive drive to organize our spiritual, political, or philosophical ideas into schools or religions, even as we claim to oppose to organized religions or fixed doctrines. It's human nature that we rush to slam shut the chapel doors or the seminary gates, so to speak, in order to ensure that our ideas, communities, or congregations remain orderly and airtight. We do this in the New Age culture as much as anyone else does.

I can think of nothing more stifling to the spiritual search than to settle upon a fixed doctrine and then decide who's in and who's out. I try to watch out for that tendency in my own work. I find that it occurs among even some of us who love the ideas of Neville or any other spiritual figures. People sometimes approach me online saying things like, "You read Tarot cards. Neville didn't believe in reading Tarot cards." Or, "Neville said not to venerate images. Yet you have a tattoo of Neville." Personally, I believe that Neville loved his students and encouraged the widest range of possibilities in their lives.

On a different tack, people sometimes object to questioning any factual issues that relate to Neville. I might question the identity or the existence of the man named Abdullah, whom Neville identified as his teacher, or suggest that Abdullah may have been a composite. Or I might suggest that Abdullah may have been a real, though dramatized, figure like Carlos Castaneda's teacher, don Juan. On occasion people grow contentious over this issue. They cite chapter and verse to demonstrate that Abdullah had to be absolutely real, in this or that way. Although I have my own theories about Abdullah's identity and discuss some of them in my book *One Simple Idea*, as well as in this work, I do not believe that it is necessary for us to abide by everything that one of our spiritual heroes said in order to believe that that person brought extraordinary and powerful truth.

I think we should love our spiritual ancestors as adults love one another. Which is to say, we love maturely and lastingly when we acknowledge flaws or raise questions, we see shortcomings, and we understand that they're part of the whole individual. When you love without the expectation or acceptance of flaw, you set yourself up for disappointment, because, one way or another, flaws *will* appear. Flaws appeared in Moses. If your love doesn't permit that, then your perception of a person runs into treacherous terrain. (The same holds true for a theory or idea). When it does, the experience can be shattering.

This is why sometimes people who are on the politically radical left go all the way over to the radical right, or vice versa. I've witnessed this slide occur in people I know. When I ask them about it, they are often unable to take in the question. They simply don't hear it. They implicitly believe that truth appears only in the form of polarity. Some people spend their entire lives gravitating from polarity to polarity. If they are disappointed in one, they decide that truth can be found only at the other end. In such cases, I think people are searching for saviors, in the form of a ideology if not a person.

I don't see Neville Goddard as a savior. But I do see him as an extraordinary figure whose simple, radical ideas have opened doors in my life that I never thought would appear.

Let me start with a basic explanation of who Neville was. The man called Neville, who wrote and spoke under his first name (his surname was Goddard), was a British-Barbadian writer, thinker, and mystic born in the West Indies in 1905. He had one essential and radical teaching, which is: *your imagination is God*. Therefore everything you see, feel, and experience is ultimately self-created and self-generated.

Neville meant that in the most literal sense. He didn't mean that your imagination is metaphorically God; he meant that *you*, the individual, *are* the Creator clothed in flesh, and that everything within your world, everything within your experience, is the outpicturing of your own emotionalized thoughts and mental images. Which is to say that even this experience that you are having right now, reading or listening to these words, is self-created. I, as Mitch, am not here; I do not exist in the sense that I am a figment of your own intellect. These ideas are *your* ideas. They are now being outpictured and experienced by you. They only seem to be coming from me, perhaps because this may be a useful time for you to encounter them. I'm simply the mental concretization of what you're already thinking about.

Neville taught that whenever in Scripture you encounter a reference to Christ or God, you're encountering a symbolic reference to and representation of your own imagination. He viewed

Scripture as an illumined book written by Eastern masters in a symbolic language, which resists ordinary literal interpretation. Across thousands of lectures and writings, Neville argued for this idea with tremendous persuasiveness.

Neville further insisted that nothing that occurs in Scripture is actual history. There's no historical truth whatsoever in Scripture: everything that appears in both the Old and New Testaments—although there are chapters of greater and lesser worth in terms of the human experience and psychological and mystical insight—is a symbolic telling of the unfoldment of your own psychic development. The earliest seeds of human self-development appear in the Old Testament and reach fruition in the New Testament, where the figure of Christ is a representation of *you*, the individual, entering awareness of the mystical and creative capacities of your mind, being crucified on the cross of awareness, and finally being resurrected into realization of yourself as the Creator.

On the cross, Christ experiences forgetfulness, asking, "Why have you forsaken me?"—just as you and I experience forgetfulness of ourselves as God until we are awakened, or resurrected, into illumined awareness. Neville taught that this process awaits all of us and that we begin to enter into it through the exercise and experience of the causative powers of the imagination. This begins to lift the veil and invites further awareness.

Neville said that Great Creation or the Great Overmind (those are my terms, not his) created men and women. Out of ultimate love for this creation, this being deliberately forgot its own deific identity and entered completely into flesh and human consciousness. Consequently, all of us are on a Christlike journey to return to an awareness of our divine nature. This begins with an awareness of the power of your own mind, and it culminates in actual, tactile experiences of yourself as God the Creator.

Inherent in Neville's point of view is a dramatic sense of self-responsibility. This aspect of his thought is both very interesting and very challenging. If you take his ideas as true, or at as a starting point for your own experimentation, they confront you with the possibility that everything that transpires in your existence is self-created. And so it follows that everything can also be changed. Neville's outlook is the ultimate expression of philosophical idealism. His ideas are tantalizing, because they suggest that any alteration you wish to bring into your life—intimate, relational, financial, career-related, artistic—lies directly within the powers of your psyche, specifically your mental pictures and emotionalized thoughts.

In Neville's system, you don't have to depend upon anybody else. You don't have to solicit things from other people. You don't have to worry about what your boss or your spouse or your boyfriend or girlfriend thinks. You possess an absolute ability to go into the silent confines of your own psyche and create the world that you wish to experience through your own use of mental scenes and feeling states.

This was Neville's teaching. Those of you who have heard him speak—many of his lectures are now online—and those of you who have read his books or transcripts of his lectures would probably agree that, although he restated this thesis thousands of times during his career (which publicly began in the late 1930s and went up until his death in 1972), his message always sounded fresh. His ideas, however often restated, always sounded vital and filled with possibility. There was something extraordinary in this. There really was something that went beyond the normal in Neville's ability to work that kind of a spell on the reader or listener. I have detected that ability in philosopher Ralph Waldo Emerson (1803–1882), mystic Jiddu Krishnamurti (1895–1986), and a very few other modern figures.

I have probably listened to hundreds of Neville's lectures. Out of great foresight and generosity, he freely permitted people to record and circulate his talks. Of course, handheld tape recorders didn't become common until the late 1960s, so many of the talks we have from Neville were delivered from that time to the end of his life. At this point, hundreds of his recordings and transcripts are online right now.

As it happened, Neville didn't renew the copyrights on any of his books (in many cases he didn't live long enough to do so), so almost all of them are in the public domain. Hence there's a huge body of public-domain material that has outlived the man's physical form by decades, and people are newly discovering it. As I was saying, I have listened to hundreds of Neville lectures at this point in my life; I've transcribed Neville's lectures for books; I have read and reread all of Neville's books; I've assembled many of his talks into anthologies, some of which are already published, some of which are forthcoming. Others who study Neville have gone further than me. But I have tried to track down the majority of available media that came out of his career, and as I've said, I've never have heard the man repeat himself in a stale way or restate his thesis in a manner that sounded rehearsed or like a stump speech. I find that remarkable.

Neville spoke without hesitation, at considerable length, and without notes. His voice flowed with mellifluous perfection. He had a masterful power of recall, so that he could refer to or recite Scriptural passages right out of the ether. He also spoke with a beautiful, clipped British-American accent. It's sometimes called a mid-Atlantic accent. It used to be more common; you don't hear it much anymore. Some people consider it affected. I do not. I think it's a beautiful way of speaking. You heard it in the actors Cary Grant, Katherine Hepburn, and Sidney Poitier, and in the writers Norman Mailer, Irving Howe, and William F. Buckley Jr. I once conversed with the American opera singer Jessye Norman, and she spoke in that way. It was lovely.

Neville spoke this way partly out of refinement and partly because he grew up on the island of Barbados, where he was born to a British Anglican family. It was a large family of nine sons and one daughter. He grew up in this West Indies atmosphere, where, as he described it, opportunities were quite limited. One's social circle and family circle were quite small. It was a tightly knit and insular society. The tropical climate and natural landscape might have been beautiful, but the social, educational, and commercial opportunities were tightly circumscribed.

In the early 1920s, at around the age of seventeen, Neville came to the United States to study theater, which was a remarkable thing for a young person from the Caribbean to do. Entirely on his own, this teenager boarded a steamer and crossed the Atlantic to make his home in New York City, where he enrolled in drama classes. In his first class, as he described it, there was a very cruel instructor, who called him to the front for the room to embarrass him and make an example of him. She asked him to speak and give a short address to the class. It's difficult for us to understand this today, but when Neville was young, and speaking in his British-island dialect, he might have sounded strange and even outlandish to American listeners at that time. (I suspect that his accent grew more clipped and refined as he aged; the mid-Atlantic accent that you hear him use in the late 1960s and early 1970s probably reflects Neville as an older man. He may have sounded a bit different when he was young.) In any event, the teacher called him up and cruelly asked him to say a few words to the class. After he did, she announced, "Now this is a man who will never earn a living using his voice."

Neville later said, "When she did that to me, she was attempting to make me into the class goat"—in other words, to hold him up as a backwoods kid who didn't belong there. Who knows why certain teachers do things like that? But I suspect we've all had them. Neville, however, was undeterred. "She didn't know the kind of man she was dealing with," he said. Rather than shrinking in embarrassment, he determined that his speaking voice would become immaculate and that he would one day earn a living using his voice.

Look at what happened. If you listen to any of Neville's lectures online, I think you'll agree that hearing his speaking voice is almost like listening to angels sing. It's beautiful and melodious, and it resounds with culture and richness. It reflects everything that I wanted to be as a child, growing up in my own backwater in eastern Queens in New York City. It wasn't exactly the capital of culture or metaphysics, and there was a lot of hostility toward people who loved such things. There was a gravitational pull to stay in your lane. This is one of the many ways in which what you or others perceive as your weakness can actually become your greatest strength. Never forget that. Others may identify something in you that seems vulnerable, but it becomes the focal point of all your efforts.

Before he became a lecturer, Neville experienced some success as an actor and stage performer. He appeared in movies, which in those days were still silent, so in another rebuke to his teacher, he didn't even have to use his voice on screen at the time. A Hollywood entertainment columnist called him the new Rudolph Valentino, the silent era's romantic leading man. Neville wasn't quite the new Valentino, but he was very handsome and poised and possessed great presence as an actor and dancer.

Neville had an angular, dashing appearance, every bit the images of a 1930s matinee star, and he retained his looks and his slender figure as he aged. Nevertheless, he rarely permitted his photograph to be taken. He wasn't a publicity hound. He displayed no vanity. If you put Neville's name into a Google image search, you'll come across the same three or four photos again and again. A couple of personal snapshots that people took of him have also appeared online lately. I've posted a couple, but they're quite rare. Until very recently, you could find only one or two images of him at all.

In 1946, Neville wrote a pamphlet called *The Search*, and a photograph of him appears in the frontispiece. In that work, he described himself as a "Magician of the Beautiful," which I chose as the title of this book. I copied that image and put it up online. There was a *Los Angeles Times* article about Neville from 1951, which included a sepia newsprint photo, and I put that up online too. Beyond these, there were really just about two pictures of Neville. This fact runs contrary to the world that we live in today. Today people traffic heavily in their image, and if somebody is a celebrity or has ambitions in that direction, there are endless photos of them. Of course, I'm talking about an earlier era, when nobody had smartphones; regardless, Neville, handsome as he was, sat for very few professional photographs.

As I was saying, Neville did experience success on screen and stage. He also appeared on Broadway. He was a ballroom dancer. He toured as part of a dance troupe in the United States and Europe.

Yet his existence was financially precarious, and this fact deeply troubled him. During lean times, he had to work as a shipping clerk and an elevator operator. He said he'd earn money one month, treat friends lavishly to meals and nights out, and then go bust. Despite the modest success he enjoyed in these professions, as the years went by, he found it all personally unsatisfying.

In the late 1920s and early 1930s, he began to study different metaphysical and occult ideas. As he told it, he bopped around different occult and mystical groups and different self-styled Rosicrucian circles, but he didn't really find anything. He tried all kinds of practices in order to heighten his sense of control over himself and his realization of the invisible world and to come into relation to some higher force or power. His practices ran to sexual abstinence, vegetarianism, and ascetic lifestyles. But here too he found nothing.

In 1931, a tremendous change occurred in Neville's life. He had a friend, a Catholic priest, who told him, "There's a man named Abdullah, whom you must go meet. He's a black Jewish man who wears a turban, and he's Ethiopian-born." As it was described, Abdullah taught a form of mysticism that follows an ancestry back to early Afro-Hebraic teachings, which now circulate in Ethiopia, but are not widely known in other parts of the world.

Neville described this priest as someone who had possessed a great deal of family money but through foolish investments in the stock market had squandered it all away. So Neville didn't place much stock in his friend. In fact he said, "I felt the man was a complete moron."

As a result, for several months Neville resisted going to meet Abdullah, but finally, after his friend continued to urge him, he agreed. Neville walked into a lecture room in New York City in 1931 and saw a very stern, regal-looking black man—turbaned, just as his friend had told him— who was preparing to present a talk to the people there. Abdullah picked Neville out immediately and said, "Neville, you are six months late."

Neville later said, "I am six months late? I never saw this man before. And I asked him what he meant."

Abdullah replied, "Neville, the brothers told me that you were coming, and you're six months late."

Neville and Abdullah became close friends as student and teacher, and they spent the next five years studying Kabbalah, Scripture, Hebrew, number symbolism, and Abdullah's mental metaphysics of the causative properties of the mind.

I'll return later to the question of who Abdullah was. Was there an Abdullah? Where did all this come from? There is a long pedigree in American metaphysics of a seeker referring to a hidden fraternity or coming under tutelage to an intriguing yet unknown teacher. Is Abdullah part of this American mythos?

Actually the presence of a black Jewish man in a turban, teaching mind metaphysics in New York City in the early 1930s, is not as strange as it may sound. First of all, at this time a philosophy called Ethiopianism had emerged in Africa, Europe, and America. A precursor to Rastafarianism, it taught that a lost tribe of Israel had found its way to Ethiopia (which is very likely true). Some teach that this tribe had, as part of its tradition and outlook, a mental metaphysics, a mystical teaching about the power of mind causation. As I've written in *Occult America*, *One Simple Idea,* and elsewhere, Marcus Garvey, the pioneering black nationalist, who was himself a precursor to both Ethiopianism and Rastafarianism (which today venerates him as something of a John the Baptist figure), had a definite, identifiable teaching of mind metaphysics in his own philosophy. This emerges in Garvey's speeches and public statements, which I've considered elsewhere.

The musical director of Marcus Garvey's Universal Negro Improvement Association (UNIA) in Harlem was a figure named Arnold Josiah Ford. If you put this name into Google, you will find photographs of a man who fits the image of Abdullah that Neville described; furthermore, Ford described himself as a black man of authentic Jewish descent. Ford appears in only a few records, but he was an absolutely real person, and I've written about him several times.

Ford too was part of the Ethiopianism movement, sometimes also called the Black Israelite movement, and he was one of the few figures in that movement who possessed a working knowledge of Hebrew. Ford also studied and taught Kabbalah in Harlem and other parts of New York City. He lived in the city at a time that intersected with Neville's years there—although he also left New York before the end of the five years of study that Neville said they had engaged in.

Soon after Haile Selassie was crowned as emperor of Ethiopia in 1930, he extended land grants to African-Americans, because he too placed stock in the teachings of Ethiopianism, although in a more nationalistic way. Like Garvey, he foresaw the emergence of a pan-African world power, which would have its seat in Ethiopia, one of Africa's most populous nations. Hence Haile Selassie wanted African-Americans to migrate to Ethiopia.

This was part of the Ethiopianism vision, and Haile Selassie extended land grants to promote it. Arnold Josiah Ford was one of a handful of people here in New York City who took up the emperor's offer. I've found records of this fact, including census data and newspaper articles. As I mention in *One Simple Idea* and elsewhere, this information shows Ford journeying to Ethiopia and settling there in 1931, the same year that he and Neville would have met.

It must have been hard for Ford, who had lived a metropolitan life, to uproot himself and move to an agrarian countryside, where life must have been comparatively difficult. He died in 1935, only shortly before Mussolini's Fascist troops crossed the Ethiopian border and invaded the nation.

This will give you an idea of why I admire these figures so much. For men like Ford and Marcus Garvey and Neville, Ethiopianism wasn't just an abstract idea, something to talk about or debate. They lived it. That's where their greatness came from. They lived from the inner light of ideas. Think how rare it is today for any of us to embrace an idea, not just in some dilettantish manner, but as a way of life.

It isn't that these great figures were correct about everything. It isn't that they cannot be criticized. It isn't that they didn't commit acts of foolishness. It's rather that they knew what it meant to place themselves fully on the line for the ideas that they believed in. They stood for something.

My theory is that Arnold Josiah Ford was Neville's Abdullah. I cannot make the final leap of stating that as a fact, because there is incongruity in the timeline. Ford left New York City in 1931, before the end of the period when Neville said that he and Abdullah had studied together.

Another possibility is that Abdullah was a composite of different teachers with whom Neville came into contact, of whom Ford was one. As a term of affection, Neville used to call Abdullah "Ab." You can hear this in certain lectures. In Arabic and Hebrew, father is "Abba," and you might also call father "Ab." He might have been tipping his hand that Abdullah was a kind of composite father figure, but that's just conjecture. It's also possible that the scenario was a kind of self-devised personal mythology, as is sometimes said about Castaneda's relationship with his legendary teacher, don Juan. (As a matter of fact, Castaneda's wife, Margaret Runyan, was a close student of Neville's.) But even that answer doesn't cover all the bases.

Joseph Murphy, another mind-metaphysics teacher and the author of the very popular 1963 book *The Power of Your Subconscious Mind*, also figures into the Abdullah narrative. In 1981, toward the end of his life, Murphy gave a series of interviews to a French priest from Quebec, which were published in a French-language book in Canada. In those interviews, Murphy said that Abdullah had been his teacher. He also said that when they first met in the 1930s Abdullah had disclosed some deeply private, intimate facts about Murphy's Irish childhood to him; for Murphy, this showed that the man possessed extrasensory abilities. So there is this one corroboration of the existence of Abdullah.

I've also visited the apartment building on West 72nd Street in New York City in which Neville said Abdullah lived, and I've been inside the common areas. Neville said that the Morgenthau family,

who were very politically and financially promi-
nent, had rented the apartment to Abdullah. I've
met at least one family member and the family historian for the Morgenthaus but have been unable
to corroborate that claim.

Some people have said to me, "If there was a
man like Abdullah circulating throughout New
York City in the early 1930s, wouldn't there be
some record of him in the press? Wouldn't people
have written about him?" I have to concede that,
yes, there is an absence of coverage. Hence I think
the answer is never going to fully disclose itself.
It's always going to remain this tantalizing historical mystery. Who was Abdullah? Was there an
Abdullah?

As I noted, Neville said that after their first
encounter, he and Abdullah studied together for
five years. But Neville said that it wasn't until the
Christmas season of 1933 that his earliest ideas
crystallized about the creative powers of the mind.
As Neville told it, he made money in the theater
one year and then he would spend it very quickly.
He'd go through constant boom-and-bust cycles.
In December 1933, he was not only financially
down-and-out, but he hadn't been back home to
Barbados for about eleven or twelve years. He

considered himself a failure in his family's eyes, and he was embarrassed to be in touch with them or ask for help. Yet he was aching to get out of the slushy, freezing cold of a New York winter and return home to spend Christmas with his family. He wanted to be reunited with his brothers, and he wanted to spend glorious months idling in the Barbadian tropics.

Abdullah said to him, "Neville, you must walk the streets of Manhattan as if you are in Barbados—and so you shall be." The teacher insisted that his student had to walk through the gray, slushy streets of upper Manhattan imagining that he was on the shady, coconut-lined lanes of his island home.

Neville tried this for two weeks. Then he went to back to Abdullah and said, "Ab, I have been trying and trying, and it's simply not working. I'm getting nowhere."

Abdullah said to him, "Neville, I can't see you. You're in Barbados," and slammed the door in his face. This was the kind of tough-love relationship they had. Neville said he felt shocked and dejected, but he continued to try. Then he said that one day out of the blue, days before Christmas, a telegram arrived at his apartment. It was from his older brother, Victor, who had written, "It's been far too long since we as a family have been together for Christmas. I have booked passage for you on the last ship leaving New York City for the West Indies." Victor enclosed $50 and said, "If you need a suit of clothes, go buy a suit of clothes. And if you're drinking, I have arranged for you to have first-class passage, and you will have the use of the bar."

Neville went down to the ship office to pick up his ticket, and the clerk told him, "Mr. Goddard, it happens that we're overbooked for first-class. We do have a reservation for you, but it's in steerage. It's in third-class. You will have access to the first class decks and dining room, but you will have to sleep in third-class quarters. When we get to St. John, you can then switch to first-class."

Neville said, "I was in no mood to argue. I was thrilled. And I went back and told Abdullah."

Abdullah expressed consternation toward him again and said, "Neville, who said you're traveling steerage? You're in Barbados, and you traveled there first-class." Again he slammed the door on him.

So Neville once more went into this feeling state, which I'm going to describe for you so that you can experiment with it yourself. When Neville returned to the shipping office on the day he was to depart, the clerk told him, "Good news, Mr. Goddard. We had a last-minute cancellation, and you're now traveling first-class all the way."

Neville said that all these events lined up in ways that were unfathomable and that he went on to spent three glorious months in Barbados. The experience solidified his personal validation of everything that Abdullah was teaching. By the late 1930s, Neville began his own career as a writer and speaker, and in 1939 he published his first book, a short, powerful work called *At Your Command*, in which he outlined his basic philosophy.

He wrote ten books until his death in 1972, and he delivered hundreds upon hundreds of lectures and radio talks. For two seasons in the mid-1950s, he had a television show in Los Angeles. He would simply sit at a table and speak, the way that Zen teacher Alan Watts did on his own contemporaneous show on public television in San Francisco. Although there were twenty-six shows in all, there exists only one single audio recording of one of them. That's all we have; we have no films or kinescopes. I spent a long time transcribing the recording (it took some doing because it's of poor quality; at times I had to struggle to complete the sentences). The transcription appears in a Neville anthology called *Infinite Potential*. It is the only transcript that I know of one of his television talks. I wish we had all of them.

I spent hours transcribing the talk, not only because of the quality of Neville's ideas but because it captures him still speaking in that somewhat rounded, countrified Barbadian-British accent. He's not always easy to understand, but this is among the most valuable pieces of anthologizing work I've ever done, because when you transcribe someone's words, you get into the guts of what they're saying; you get into the experience of it. And Neville told illustrative stories from his life with such sincerity and freshness that no matter how many times I hear the same story, I always discover something new.

In this particular episode, Neville told two stories. One was about securing a steamer ticket to leave Barbados at another time, when he and his wife and daughter were at risk of being stranded there for months. The other was about a blind young woman from San Francisco who had lost all means of commuting to her job after a change in city bus routes. Having exhausted all other options, she used the mental exercise of imagining herself being chauffeured to and from her job. Very shortly afterward, two local men volunteered, as a matter of good will, to drive her on her commute to and from work. One of them was a salesman for a liquor company. He said that although he made a very good living, he had never given anything back to the community, so this was his opportunity to make a contribution.

Neville pointed out that we all have our roles to play in life, whether so-called saint or sinner, hero or antihero, public figure or private person, benefactor or thief—each of us is fated, or at least suited, to those pivotal moments where we serve our critical function within the mental order of things to bridge the gap between imagination and lived experience. We are all devising our own imaginary universes, and we crisscross into one another's existence at needed moments, like an infinitely dimensional mosaic uniting a universal dream of life. This was Neville's metaphysics.

ECCE HOMO

2

Often I become interested in a philosophy because of the person behind it. I respond to the person first and to his or her ideas second. Frankly, I do not believe in the principle, which was often repeated back in my publishing days, that you must separate the message from the messenger. We said this in spiritual publishing because the teachers and visionaries with whom we worked so often proved disappointing in person. We would strive, not always successfully, to remind ourselves that the message was valid even if the teacher was dispiriting in behavior or temperament. But I no longer abide by that principle. I believe that I should live out the philosophy that I am espousing. If I am not, there's a flaw in me or in the ideas I'm working with. This doesn't mean that someone won't make grave mistakes, or do foolish or selfish things, but one way or another, I want to know how an idea is really impacting a person's life, and I try to be transparent about that in my own life. That's why I don't like those rehearsed-sounding fifteen-minute answers. They don't seem lived. But I felt there was something unified in Neville's life and teachings, so I responded to that impression.

I first discovered Neville in the summer of 2003. It was a fitful period for me, because I hadn't been writing for years. I had begun my career as a journalist, but journalism, or at least daily journalism, just wasn't for me, so I went into book publishing. I was frustrated here too. It was good to me financially, and I had my successes, but I was never really in love with it. I felt as if I didn't stand for anything. I often felt as if my colleagues and I were just throwing ideas up against a wall, seeing whatever would stick and often publishing things more to fill a ledger than out of any deep-seated passion. I later emerged from this period and felt dedicated to my program of metaphysical literature; but this was the feeling for some years.

In the summer of 2003, however, something pivotal occurred. The editors of *Science of Mind* magazine approached me. They had gotten Major League pitcher Barry Zito, who was a very big sports star then, to agree to an interview. Barry used various mind-metaphysics methods, including the ideas of Neville, Ernest Holmes, and Joseph Murphy, as part of his training regimen, and he agreed to discuss this with the magazine.

Barry came from a Southern California family that had founded a spiritual movement called Teachings of the Inner Christ, which has ideas and a theology that are similar to Neville's. Barry's mother, Roberta, and his father, Joe, were both leaders in the movement, and this was very much a part of Barry's upbringing. He was one of the top young pitchers in the league, winning the Cy Young Award, and he was an All-Star. He was also known as a dedicated metaphysical seeker, which was and remains rare in the world of pro baseball. Because of that, journalists and others would sometimes make fun of him, calling him Planet Zito or Captain Quirk.

So here was this star athlete who was very public about his metaphysical commitments, and an interview with him was a very big coup for *Science of Mind*. They wanted to bring the opportunity to someone they felt could trust to turn the interview into a first-rate feature article. I felt honored that they brought the opportunity to me and was determined not to disappoint them.

I conducted a substantial phone interview with Barry in the late summer of 2003, and we remained friendly for some time after that. At one point, when we were discussing various spiritual questions and practices, he said to me, "Wow, you must really be into Neville." I had never heard the name. He was incredulous and said, "Oh, you would love him."

As soon as we got off the phone, I got a 1966 book of Neville's called *Resurrection*. It was the last full-length book that he published. I completely fell into it. You have no doubt had your own moments when you meet someone or read something and realize that you've encountered a seismic influence in your life. I immediately felt a sense of solidity about him as a person. There was a seriousness about him, a refinement, a fibrousness of character. I never looked back.

After reading *Resurrection*, I found out whatever I could about Neville. Reading his works and listening to and transcribing his talks gave me an indelible sense that this man was offering me a radical theory that he had lived out in his own life. And that, finally, is the only thing that I really care about. I've reached a point in my search where I'm not persuaded by anything that anybody tells me until I see it demonstrated in his or her conduct. Like many of you, I've had experiences of somebody who calls himself a spiritual activist or some such, yet who loses his temper at the slightest infringement or inconvenience; or somebody who has dedicated decades to meditation but who yells at a waiter or cabdriver because of some minor frustration. I personally know people who tell me that they tithe but in fact do not tithe, or do so irregularly. (I'm agnostic on that practice—I do not endorse it one way or another. I've tried it personally, and it's not for me, but I do not discount the experience of tithing for prosperity.) Hence at this point in my search, I don't care what anybody says; I want to see what they actually do. And I brought this same sensibility to my study of Neville. I now want to tell you just a wild but true story about where that went.

MIND IN ACTION

3

Neville would sometimes make claims in his talks, and I would ask myself, "Could these be true?" I decided to follow up on one of the most fantastic of them, and I'll tell you what I found.

Neville was drafted into the U.S. Army in November 1942. He was already in his late thirties at that time, so he was a little old, but during World War II, men could be drafted up to the age of forty-five. The Army was very concerned about sufficient troop levels, so there were a lot of draftees of different ages, and he was among them.

Neville's basic training was at Camp Polk, Louisiana. As he put it, "I wanted no part of this war." He wanted to return back home to his apartment in Greenwich Village, where he was newly married and had a newborn daughter, Victoria, or Vicky, who lives in Los Angeles today. (Vicky doesn't speak publicly about her father, and I've been unsuccessful in my attempts to reach her, but she did wish me good luck on a Neville anthology, and I was touched by that.) Neville was eager to get out of military service, so he went to his commanding officer and requested an honorable discharge. The commanding officer said to him, "Of course not. Get back to your barracks."

Neville returned to his barracks, but he recalled, "I wasn't dejected. For several weeks, every single night, I would go to sleep on my Army cot, and I would imagine myself back in Greenwich Village, walking through Washington Square Park, walking through the streets that I knew back home."

The building where Neville lived is still standing. It's a beautiful art-deco apartment tower on Washington Square West. Today New York University owns the building and maintains it as residential apartments. It looks out over Washington

Square Park. It is the same address that appears on Neville's draft card.

Neville would go to sleep on his Army cot and physically picture himself strolling the tree-lined paths of Washington Square Park back in Greenwich Village, back in his apartment, very comfortably, very naturally, feeling that he was at home. For several weeks, he would drift to sleep each night picturing and feeling himself physically—not just seeing himself, but really *feeling* himself in a tactile sense—walking around his home and seeing things from the perspective of being there. He would fall asleep in this vision.

Eventually his commanding officer called him back into his office and said, "Goddard, do you still want a discharge?"

He said, "Yes, I do."

The C.O. said, "Well, you have it. You can go back home."

And Neville said, "Off I went."

I read this and thought, "That doesn't wash. Why would the U.S. Army honorably discharge a healthy, sinewy dancer at the height of the war effort, just for the asking—for no apparent reason? This sounds suspicious."

I decided to research this question and make it into a test case. I have Neville's draft card, and I found his surviving Army records. They include his final pay stub, which is dated four months from when he was initially drafted. He was honorably discharged in March 1943, and the reason given on his pay stub is: "discharged from service to accept employment in an essential wartime industry." No other reason was given.

Oddly, in September 1943, several months after Neville's return, he was profiled in *The New Yorker*—not a magazine typically known for its occult enthusiasms. The profile describes him all around town, speaking uptown at the Actors' Church, speaking downtown, delivering his talks to starry-eyed, often female, audiences. The reporter seemed to find him an unusual, likable, and somewhat bizarre figure.

Neville is one of the few occult or mystical figures who has received this kind of extended treatment in *The New Yorker*. The article clearly demonstrated that Neville was back in town and on the metaphysical speaking circuit—but still I couldn't figure out why the Army would have discharged him.

I got in touch with an Army public-affairs spokesman and I laid all this out. I said, "You

know, this man's job was as a metaphysical lecturer, but his final pay stub says he was discharged
to return to a vital civilian occupation. How does
this qualify?"

The spokesman responded, "That's all the information we have. Unfortunately, one year after Mr.
Goddard's death, his records were destroyed in a
fire at one of our recordkeeping facilities."

So I don't know precisely what transpired, but
I can tell you that, at least logistically, the trail
matches up with what Neville described. The tim-
ing matches up as well. I only know that he spoke
earnestly about using his metaphysical methods
and gaining a completely unlikely honorable discharge four months after his induction.

I found similar paper trails confirming things
that Neville said about his family. When he was
growing up, the Goddard family ran a small gro-
cery business in Barbados that developed into
a large international catering and food-service
company, today called Goddard Industries.
They're active throughout the Caribbean and
Latin America, supplying food for cruise ships,
hotels, and public and industrial facilities. For
years in his lectures, Neville spoke about his family's dramatic rise.

In short, there were a number of things Neville described that matched up with the time line and logistics. You can draw your own conclusions about the soundness of his ideas and what was going on internally in him, but my conviction is that he reported the events of his life with traceable veracity. And that's meaningful, because I believe that people should put themselves on the line for their ideas and express them in their own conduct. I also believe there must be a high standard of verifiable reportage, because we're describing and endorsing methods that at least some listeners will adopt themselves.

I think that if we're serious about what we're doing, those of us who are interested in the extra-physical, the parapsychological, and the spiritual ought to create reliable records and hold ourselves to a high standard of truth. If I exaggerate or distort something—and plenty of this goes on in writings by metaphysical ministers and successful New Age authors—what am I doing but leading people into a fog of delusion?

In matters of ultimate truth, it is a terrible disservice for a writer or speaker to exaggerate, to dramatize, to create composite characters simply in order to heighten the drama or highlight their claims of exceptionality. With these subjects, we must avoid playing games, getting fuzzy around the edges, or making things sound more exceptional than they really are because we think, "I'm not able to relate *every* story, so in this one I'm entitled to juice things up a little." I don't think we should tolerate that. My judgment is that Neville told the truth, and that's meaningful to me.

THE METHOD

4

Everything that I've just described demonstrates that Neville was a remarkable personage—charismatic and deeply appealing. His philosophy has an obvious magnetism about it. The idea of being able to reshape your own life without depending upon anybody else is, in principle, exciting and powerful. But there's only one question on which all of it stands: *Does it work?*

Neville would always tell audiences, "Test me, test me, prove me wrong. Try my ideas. Do it tonight, this very night. If I'm wrong, forget you

ever heard my name." I've always loved that quality about him.

He would evangelize for his ideas, but he
wouldn't proselytize. He wasn't just interested in
counting noses at events or selling books. When
his talks grew more esoteric in nature, a speaking agent warned him to return to more conven-
tional, law-of-attraction style themes or he'd lose
his audience. "Then I'll speak it to the bare walls,"
Neville replied. If someone didn't want his ideas,
he wouldn't try to rope them in. This is a mark of
confidence in one's methods.

You can use several different techniques in
connection with Neville's ideas, and, as he did,
I challenge you to try them and see what happens. You're entitled to results. I believe strongly
in results. I believe that every therapeutic and
ethical and spiritual philosophy should result in
some concrete change and improvement in your
life or your conduct; if it doesn't, then such an
idea should have no hold on you. I feel similarly
strongly that the ability to describe a concrete
outcome in your life is vitally important, and that
too was always part of Neville's teaching. Testimony is both an important source of ideas and an
invitation to others.

One way of using Neville's approach to mental creativity is to enter into an inner state of theatrical or childlike make-believe. Not childish but child*like*: a state of internal wonder and pretending. Children are so good at this. We get embarrassed about this quality as we age, but Neville talked about walking the streets of Manhattan imagining that he was in the tree-lined lanes of Barbados, boarding a ship to some desired destination, or in a location where he wanted to be.

He would say: "Unfoldment will come. You will see." He would always say that an assumption, although false, if persisted in, eventually hardens into fact. He would say, "Assume the state of the wish fulfilled. Live from the end. Live from the state of your wish fulfilled." Remember, Neville would remind listeners, you're not in a state of *wanting*; you're in a state of *having received*. Your aim is simply to occupy the emotional and mental state that you would experience after having received.

Abdullah didn't say, "Neville, you *will be* in Barbados." He said, "Neville, you *are* in Barbados." Abdullah didn't say, "Neville, you *will* travel first-class." He said, "Neville, you *are* in Barbados, and you *traveled* first-class." Living from the end means adopting the feeling state of already having received the desired thing. I have the words "Live from the end" tattooed on my left upper arm. It's a mnemonic device.

One simple way to use Neville's method is to freely enter this state of make-believe, as you used to when you were a child. Of course, you must also continue to go about your adult life in this world of Caesar and currency and commerce, and fulfill your obligations and do the things you need to do. You cooperate with the world. You must abide by the world. You must do the things that the world needs you to do. But the secret engine behind what's really going on is what you're imagining. Within are the hidden currents of emotionalized thought, which are the actual engine of what's occurring.

How long will it take you to see your desired changes in outer life? How long will it take for outer life to conform to your internal focus, your living from the end of your ideal? It took Neville several weeks to produce what he wanted in connection with Barbados. It also took him several weeks to get his honorary discharge.

This question of time intervals has recently become very hot for me personally, because with all the stresses that life throws at us, it is not easy to adopt a feeling state and stick with it for weeks. It's very difficult, in part because the world we live in does everything possible to disrupt our inner quietude—more so today than it did even in Neville's time. Everything conspires to interrupt us. If you're silent, people think there's something wrong with you. If you're standing in an elevator in your apartment building and you're not humming or whistling or complaining or commenting on the weather or looking at your phone, people think there's something strange going on. Every one of our relationships, every one of our workplaces, everywhere you go, robs us of our quietude. You walk into a pizza parlor or a bar or a restaurant, and the television is blaring. You go to your optician or dentist, and there's a television blaring in the waiting area.

We've been conditioned to think that it's a relief to constantly have noise going on. A relief from what? A relief from the actual experience of living—and from living within. We all participate in this. Notice how we force children to talk. We think it's cute. Every time a young child is playing or is in their presence, people pester the child to say something. The child senses that many of the questions put his or her way are rhetorical or frivolous and appropriately ignores them. But we lose that quality as we age. We are miseducated to speak constantly and frivolously—usually about nothing. We think silence is pathology. So it is very difficult to maintain a make-believe or feeling state within.

One of Neville's gifts was that he was able to maintain this state. I don't think he quite grasped that this gift didn't come naturally to all of us. Remember, he was a stage actor, a performer: he had a natural inclination in that direction. For those of us who are not actors, it's more difficult to enter into that royal road of inner pretending, but it's easier if you select a goal about which you're really passionate. In my experience, you can't experiment with these ideas unless you select something for which you're really impassioned. Passion sustains the feeling state.

I have had extraordinary actualizations of out-pictured ideas in my life, but this process won't work if you approach it frivolously. If I tell myself, "I'm going to test Neville by imagining that there will be a rose on the table in my apartment sometime in the not distant future," it never works, because I really don't care one way or another whether the rose is there. But if it's something that

I'm intimately interested in, that I'm passionate for, I find the process much easier and more powerful.

I mentioned the question of a time interval. Neville noted later in his life that there could be a substantial time interval between your visioning, your mental imaging, and the appearance of the wished-for thing. He would point out that the gestation period of a human life is nine months. The gestation period of a horse is eleven months. The gestation period of a lamb is five months. The gestation period of a chick is twenty-one days. There is almost always going to be some time interval. You must persist. If you want to find yourself in Paris, and you wake up every day and you're still far away from Paris, you're naturally going to feel disappointed or dejected. But if you really stick with it, you will see that your assumptions eventually concretize into reality, and the correspondences will be uncanny.

As I mentioned, I've had such experiences in my own life; but I've personally observed that in some cases, there have been extended time intervals. This has been true regarding my career as a writer, speaker, and narrator. The philosopher Goethe made an interesting observation. We've all heard the expression "Be careful what you wish for; you just might get it." It actually has its roots in Goethe. Taking a leaf from Goethe's play *Faust*, Ralph Waldo Emerson noted this dynamic in his 1860 essay "Fate," which led to the popular adage. Emerson wrote:

> And the moral is that what we seek we shall find; what we flee from flees from us; as Goethe said, "what we wish for in youth, comes in heaps on us in old age," too often cursed with the granting of our prayer: and hence the high caution, that, since we are sure of having what we wish, we must beware to ask only for high things.

We are being warned to act with perspective: what we wish for when we are young will come upon us in waves when we are old. Many people would object to that claim, saying that they have all kinds of unfilled wishes. But unlocking the truth of this observation requires peeling back the layers of your mind and probing formative images and fantasies from when you were very young. What was the earliest dream you can remember when you first came into conscious memory, maybe at age three or four? I mean a literal nighttime dream.

I had a very particular dream, and it has an interesting congruity with one of Neville's stories. When I was four years old there was a young girl in our neighborhood, Eleanor, who was deaf. One night I dreamt—as vividly as though it were yesterday—that some bad guys had kidnaped her. I organized a crew of friends into a rescue party, and standing in a circle I told them, "We gotta save Eleanor." That dream has played out in my life in uncanny ways.

But the important thing here is *you*. What were some of your earliest dreams, memories, and mental formulations? What were your fantasies when you were very young? I do believe that children—certainly this was true of me—have a very intense fantasy lives even at age four or five. What were your earliest fantasies?

I believe that Goethe's observation relates to Neville's remarks about the passage of time and the gestation period between the thought and the actualization. If you take Goethe's counsel, you might be surprised to discover an extraordinary symmetry between the things that you're living out in your life today and things that you harbored and thought about when you were very young. These can be positive, negative, or anywhere in between.

In addition to this make-believe mindset I've been describing, there is another basic step that Neville prescribed, and it is very simple. Anybody can do it. It's nearly effortless. You can do it tonight, and I hope you will.

Neville would talk about the importance of going into a kind of natural meditative state that he described as one of relaxed drowsiness. Sleep researchers call this the hypnogogic state. It is associated with physical immobility, and you enter it just as you're drifting off to sleep at night. It's those exquisitely relaxed moments that you experience as you're hovering between sleep and conscious awareness. It's an unusually supple state, because you experience visions, fantasies, hallucinations, and even noises—yet you retain conscious control over your thoughts and cognition. This state returns in a slightly different form in the morning as you reenter awareness. In this context it is sometimes called *hypnopompia*: you're still in a dreamy, surreal frame of mind, but you can control your cognition. Thus we all go through this state twice in the twenty-four-hour cycle.

Clinical researchers of ESP have found that this hypnagogic state is prime time for psychic activity or telepathy. (This is a completely different subject, which I write about in my books *One Simple Idea* and *The Miracle Club*.) I recently spoke at a fundraiser for one of America's oldest scholarly ESP labs, the Rhine Research Center in Raleigh, North Carolina. Researchers there and elsewhere are very interested in hypnagogia. They have found that subjects in hypnagogic states show statistical spikes in anomalous transfers of information, such as "receiving" messages in an extrasensory fashion. It is a very sensitive state, and we all enter it naturally when we are drifting to sleep.

This was the state during which Neville advised using mental pictures to experience your ideal. He never talked about psychic research or neuroscience in detail, and in fact the research that I'm describing didn't occur until decades after his death. But he instinctively and experientially understood that this state of natural relaxation is very powerful.

This state of drowsy relaxation is not limited to nighttime or morning. Neville often described entering into it at about 3:00 p.m. He would have lunch, at which he would usually consume a bottle of wine. (Neville was not ascetic. He was known to be a considerable drinker. Once he said in a lecture, "Smoking, I never got. Drinking, that I got.")

The important thing is not how you get into this state, but that you enter into it and use it. When you do—and this part of the exercise should be decided beforehand—you must focus on something you want. You have something that you wish for. What is it? Do you want to finish a project? Are you looking for a certain job? Are you looking for a mate? Do you want to be married? Do you want to see yourself on stage? Do you want to see your paintings hanging in a gallery? Do you want to see someone you love at your side? Whatever it is, everyone has something. From this state of physical immobility, imagine yourself in the scene that you want to be in—some little, small drama that implies the fulfillment of what you're after. For example, let's say you want to be married. Feel the weight and the density of a wedding band on your finger. Feel yourself twisting it or turning it around.

Let's say you want public acclaim or success. You might feel the flash of cameras going off while you're standing on a red carpet or a runway. If you want a promotion in your job, you might imagine your boss shaking your hand and saying, "Congratulations."

The point is not to see this action as if it's occurring on a movie screen, as if you're watching it happen to you, but to really feel yourself *in* the action. Neville would say, "If I want to climb a ladder, I don't see myself climbing a ladder. *I climb*! I feel the density and the thickness of the rungs and my weight as I'm placing foot after foot on each rung." You want to *feel* yourself in the action.

After playing this scene out several times in your mind—as many times as feel natural—you allow yourself to drift to sleep. You do this night after night. With this method, Neville vowed that what you're imagining will eventually and unmistakably concretize in your life, and by means that you never foresaw. He specifically said not to worry about the means. The event will unfold in its own natural way. Don't do anything to precipitate it. Don't wonder, "How will this happen?" This is not a logical exercise.

This step is very difficult for me, because even though I talk about metaphysics and my life is dedicated to it, I am plagued with an excessive degree of logic. It's very helpful in some ways, it's great if you want to get from point A to point B, but this thought experiment is not logical in the traditional sense.

Neville recommends that you avoid thinking in terms of, "It will happen this way or that way" or "I'll do something to make it happen." His attitude was that the event will unfold in its own lovely, harmonious, perfect way. Your job is not to draw the map. Your job is to live from the destination.

WHY IT WORKS—
MAYBE

5

Why should these methods work at all? In *The Miracle Club* I propose a theory of mind causation. It may be wrong, it may be grossly incomplete, but I feel that we need to at least try. It's necessary, I believe, for our generation to do more than tell the same stories over and over. We must experiment, we must experience, we must testify, we must have results—and we must attempt to come up with reasons why this mind causation may work.

I'll start by quoting a remarkable thing that Neville said in 1948: "Scientists will one day explain why there is a serial universe. But in practice, how you use this serial universe to change the future is more important."

It was a striking observation, because it wasn't until years later that quantum physicists began to talk about the many-worlds theory. Physicist Hugh Everett III devised the concept in 1957. He was trying to make sense of some of the extraordinary findings that had been occurring for about three decades in quantum particle physics. For example, scientists are able to demonstrate, through various interference patterns, that a subatomic particle occupies a wave state or state of superposition—that is, an infinite number of places—until someone takes a measurement: it is only when the measurement is taken that the particle collapses, so to speak, from a wave state into a localized state. At that point it occupies a definite, identifiable, measureable place. Before the measurement is taken, the localized particle exists only in potential.

Now I have just about squeezed all of quantum physics into roughly a sentence. I think it's an accurate sentence, but obviously I'm taking huge complexities and reducing them into the dimensions of a marble. But I think I'm faithfully stating what has been observed in the last eighty-plus years of particle experiments. And we're seeing that on the subatomic scale, matter does not behave as we understand it to.

Our understanding of matter in our macro world generally comes from measuring things through our five senses, and experiencing them as singularities. There is one table. It is solid and definable. It's not occupying an infinite number of spaces. But contemporary quantum physicists have theorized that we may not normally see or experience superposition phenomena because of information leakage. This means that we gain or lose data based on the fineness of our measurement. When you're measuring things with exquisitely well-tuned instruments, like a microscope, you're seeing more and more of what's going on— and that's actual reality. But when you pan the camera back, so to speak, your measurements coarsen and you're seeing less and less of what's actually happening.

To all ordinary appearances, a table is solid. The floor beneath your feet is solid. Where you're sitting is solid. But measuring through atomic-scale microscopes, we realize that if you go deeper and deeper, you have space within these objects.

Particles make up the atom, and still greater space appears. We don't experience that; we experience solidity. But no one questions that there's space between the particles that compose an atom. Furthermore, we possess decades of data demonstrating that when subatomic particles are directed at a target system, such as a double slit, they appear in infinite places at once until a measurement is made; only then does locality appear. But we fail to see this fact unless we're measuring things with comparative exactitude. Hence what I'm describing seems unreal based on lived experience—but it's actual.

In any event, my supposition is this: if particles appear in an infinite number of places at once until a measurement is taken; and if, as we know from studying the behavior and mechanics of subatomic particles, there's an infinitude of possibilities; and if we know, as we have for many years, that time is relative, then it is possible to reason—and it's almost necessary to reason—that linearity itself, by which we organize our lives, is an illusion. Linearity is a useful and necessary device for five-sensory beings to get through life, but it doesn't stand up objectively. Linearity is a device, a subjective interpretation of what's really going on.

It's not reflected in Einstein's theory of relativity, which posits that time slows down when it begins to approach the speed of light. Nor is it reflected in quantum mechanics, where particles appear in an infinitude of places and do not obey any orderly modality. Linearity is not replicating itself when a measurement taken of a particle serves to localize the appearance or existence of the object.

If we pursue this line of thought further—and this is where the many-worlds theory comes into play—the very decision to take a measurement (or even not to take a measurement) not only localizes a particle but creates a past, present, and future for that particle. The decision of an observer to take a measurement creates a multidimensional reality for the particle.

So whatever that particle is doing, the very fact that a sentient observer has chosen to take a measurement at that time, place, moment, and juncture creates a whole past, present, future—an entire infinitude of outcomes. A different set of outcomes would exist if that measurement were never taken. A different set of outcomes would also exist if that measurement were taken one second later, or five minutes later, or tomorrow. And what is tomorrow? When particles exist in superposition until somebody takes a measurement, there is no such thing as tomorrow, other than subjectively.

And what are our five senses but a technology by which we measure things? What are our five senses but a biological technology, not necessarily different in intake from a camera, photometer, digital recorder, or microscope? So it's possible that within reality—within this extralinear, super-positioned infinitude of possibilities in which we are taking measurements—we experience things based upon our perspective.

Neville's instinct was correct in this sense. He taught that you can take a measurement by employing the visualizing forces of your own imagination. You're taking a measurement within the infinitude of possible outcomes. The measurement localizes or actualizes the thing itself. Hence his formula: an assumption, if persisted in, hardens into fact. But the assumption must be persuasive; it must be convincing. That's why the emotions and feeling states must come into play. And Neville observed that the hypnagogic state helps facilitate that process.

I believe that Neville is going to be remembered, and is being looked upon today, as having created the most elegant mystical analog to quantum physics. He was thinking and talking about these ideas long before the popularization of quantum physics. He had a remarkable instinct in the 1940s, which has been tantalizingly, if indirectly, reiterated by people studying quantum theory—people who have never heard the name of Neville. Yet it wouldn't surprise me if, within a generation or so, some physics students begin to read him as a philosophical adjunct to their work. That may sound unlikely, but remember that many of the current generation of physicists were inspired by *Star Trek* and *Zen and the Art of Motorcycle Maintenance*, and I believe there is greater openness today to questions of awareness and mind causation.

Neville was very little known when Barry Zito first mentioned him to me in 2003. Even people in the New Age culture hadn't heard of him, or only vaguely knew his name. Yet as I write these words more than fifteen years later, he is becoming remarkably well known; he has figured into some best-selling spiritual books and he has a considerable fan base online. That's a turnaround for a man who died in relative obscurity in West Hollywood in 1972.

Indeed Neville's ideas are far more widely known today than they were during his lifetime. This is obviously aided by digital technology, but above all it has to do with his vision. The fact that he naturally expressed all of these experiential insights and allowed them to be freely recorded and shared has given him great currency in our digital culture, and in the lives of a new generation of seekers. In time, I think Neville will be among the most widely read and talked about mystical figures of the last century.

We all live by philosophies, unspoken or not. Even if we say we don't have an ideology, we obviously have assumptions by which we navigate life. When I look back upon people like Neville and Abdullah, I realize that their greatness, as I suggested earlier, is that they lived by the inner light of their ideas. That is a rare trait in our world today. We are a world of talkers. People are sarcastic or cruel over Twitter, and they think they're taking some great moral stand. Is it brave for someone who lives miles away and doesn't even use his real name to call people out online? That's no victory. It's make-believe morality.

When we look back on certain figures in the political, cultural, artistic, and spiritual spheres, those we remember are the ones who lived by the inner light of their ideas, who put themselves on the line, for success or failure, based upon an idea.

My wish for every one of you reading or listening to these words is that you provide that same example. Let us make a silent pact with one another. There's no club to join. You don't have to get a membership card or declare yourself part of anything. But let's make a pact—each of us who are experiencing these words, to experiment together—and to begin doing so starting from now.

Tonight, when you go home into the privacy and interior of your own psyche, experiment with these ideas. See what you find. You don't have to share it with anybody, at least not right away; it's your private experiment. I said earlier that I believe in accurate testimony—but that's personally elective. I also believe in privacy. There's too much forced intimacy in our New Age culture. These are your ideas to try; if they work, you can elect whether to testify to them or not.

I believe in respecting the privacy of yourself and others. That's why at my events I don't make people greet each other or hug or wear name tags or anything like that. I won't speak at places where they corral workshop attendees into sharing groups or coerced intimacies. I honor your sense of discretion. So it's up to you whether to join this pact, whether to silently try those experiments, and to do so together.

And I really must say the following, and I mean this in my heart: if you sincerely attempt what I am describing, I believe that you will find greatness, because you will be making the effort to live by the inner light of an idea. That's the legacy that Neville has left us. Let's use it.

QUESTIONS AND RESPONSES

6

QUESTION: Sometimes I find myself going into the hypnagogic state right in the middle the day. Can I give into it and use it? Sometimes I've had very deep experiences and insights, even precognitive experiences, just during regular hours.

RESPONSE: Two quick things. First, it struck me that the state that you were talking about might have some similarity to the state that medical clairvoyant Edgar Cayce (1877–1945) described being in when he was healing. He entered a trance-like state, which was neither sleep nor wakefulness, about three times a day. Second, I think that when you feel yourself in that naturally relaxed, drowsy state, you should if at all possible—if you're not in traffic or somewhere that requires your attention—give into it and attempt the methods we've been discussing. There's no one time of day, or particular setting, that you're limited to. Neville would relax in an easy chair at 3 p.m. Use whatever is available.

QUESTION: You mention sarcasm. Do you know the origin of the word? It's actually from the Greek *sarkazein*, which literally means *to tear flesh*. Isn't that how you feel when someone attacks you verbally? Once you know that, you can be free of that person's projection. Just let it go. A lot of people will say, "This is terrible. Should I let it go? It's too much." I would say let everything go.

RESPONSE: I joke about it sometimes, but I actually get an extraordinarily small amount of hate online. It's remarkable, because I go on *Coast to Coast AM* or other national shows and talk about Satanism and controversial topics, but I find that many people can hear and relate to the sincerity of my questions, and they seem to respect that. Sometimes I think I'm going to get torn into, but instead I get invited on a Mormon radio show or a Seventh-day Adventist podcast, and we have a straightforward and respectful exchange about outsider topics. I've observed that I make myself easy to reach—I mean, I post my real email on my website—and I've come to feel that the fewer barriers I erect, the fewer troublemakers seem to beat a path to my door. I don't know why that is, but that's what I've observed.

QUESTION: When you appeared on Duncan Trussell's podcast, you said that you had a laminated card in your pocket with a clearly defined goal on it. I was wondering if you could share a little about that process.

RESPONSE: I use lots of such methods. I probably read about that one in Napoleon Hill's book *Think and Grow Rich*, although it's appeared in many places. I believe that you should use whatever devices you wish in order to keep your mind on track. If there's something you want to think of, whether it's a sum of money, a goal, a relationship, or an artwork—whatever you're working on that's important to you—I feel strongly that it's entirely justifiable to put a card in your pocket or paste messages up around the house. Any number of things can keep you on target, and you should be free-flowing and experimental about them. It might mean listening multiple times to a song or repeatedly viewing a movie. I've watched the movie *A Most Violent Year* several times, because the main character, Abel, is inspiring to me.

I think any form of mental and emotional opening that you can enter into is worthy. Apropos of this card you mentioned, I do believe there is a certain power in writing something down in a tactile way, whether it be a wish, an observation, or a goal, because when you've written it down, not just on a computer screen, a phone, or a tablet, but on a piece of paper or a card, you've taken the first step, however slight it may seem, toward concretizing that goal.

Writing down a goal on a piece of paper seems so small, but that decision can be meaningful. First of all, most people never do it; 99 percent of humanity doesn't do it, including those who ridicule such things. Most of us drift with our emotions or attempt to appeal to our peer groups. For most people, there's work, there's entertainment, and then there's death.

Not for us. When you take even a small step, like just writing something down on a card, you are actualizing the thing in a way that you can touch, feel, sense, see, even smell. I believe that very small steps can be revolutionary, though most people never take them. A small step can be a doorway for something to enter your life.

QUESTION: This morning I listened to a podcast about psychic development, and the teacher was suggesting paying attention—listening, smelling, and being mindful in a concentrated way of all the different ways in which you gather information, and being open to it. I did that on a crowded subway this morning, and I found that my eyes were gathering information differently than my ears. My eyes are more like a sponge—everything comes flooding in—while my ears sort of gather things. As I opened my eyes upon reaching my destination, I saw a poster that showed children playing, and it said, "Feel everything around you," or "Feel it all around you." You'd mentioned something about this, and this idea of feeling, sensing, touching, and bringing in the whole self is a nice reminder.

RESPONSE: Israel Regardie, the occult philosopher, who was at one time a secretary to Aleister Crowley, wrote a book in 1946 about mystical movements in America that he called *The Romance of Metaphysics*. He dedicated a substantial chapter to Neville. He wrote the following, and I quote it directly:

> Of all the metaphysical systems with which I am acquainted, Neville's is the most evidently magical. But being the most magical, it requires for that very reason, a systematized training on the part of those who would approach and enter its portals. It requires a dynamic alteration of viewpoint—a revolutionary turning around of the mind. An entirely new and radical attitude to life and living must be developed, not merely intellectually, but emotionally.

Regardie believed in Neville's ideas, but he said that Neville may not have realized that his readers and listeners didn't necessarily share his ability, as an actor and stage performer, to freely enter into the feeling state that he described as the key to unlocking the creative energies. As a dancer and trained performer, Neville was far more capable of adopting a physical or feeling state than the average person, and Regardie thought he might have overlooked that critical fact. He thought that Neville should have supplied more in the way of instructions and training.

Hence one of the things that I'm working on for 2020 is a new Neville anthology called *The Ideal Realized*. In that collection, I'm pulling together Neville's most practical methods. I am searching through his lectures and literature for his most hard-core instructions, because I think Regardie made a good point. I also think that over the span of his career, Neville probably did provide something like the systematized teaching that Regardie was suggesting, but in stages. It might be helpful to people, including me, to have it all in one place. I'm working on that.

Is Your Imagination God?

Three Simple Steps to Experimenting with the Ideas of Neville Goddard
By Mitch Horowitz

I recently received an ebullient letter from a barbershop owner in Lafayette, Georgia, who loves the work of mystic Neville Goddard. As a historian of the occult, I receive few fan letters from Lafayette—this one made me take special notice.

The metaphysical teacher Neville, who wrote and spoke under his first name, has been growing in popularity since his death, in 1972, and particularly in the past decade or so, when a wide range of metaphysical writers, including Rhonda Byrne and Wayne Dyer, named him as an influence. A historical profile of Neville that I wrote in

2005 has become one of my most widely read and reprinted pieces. Neville's books are entering multiple editions, and his lectures, preserved digitally from recordings that he freely allowed during his lifetime, receive hits numbering in the hundreds of thousands.

This is an unlikely renaissance for a British-Barbadian metaphysical lecturer who died in near-obscurity and whose 10 books and thousands of lectures center on one theme: *Your imagination is God*. Everything that you see and experience, Neville wrote, are your emotionalized thoughts and mental images pushed out into the world. The God of Scripture, he taught, is simply a metaphor of your own creative faculties, and your surrounding world is self-formed in the most literal sense.

Neville promulgated ideas that one immediately wants to argue with or wave off—but this is where the writer differs from most of the mystical thinkers of the previous century. In his books, pamphlets, and lectures, Neville argued for this radical thesis with extraordinary precision, vividness, and persuasiveness. With his appealing mid-Atlantic accent, encyclopedic command of Scripture, and gentle yet epics peaking style, Neville could, in the space of a 20-minute lecture, upend your entire view of life. Humanity, he taught, does not respond to circumstances—rather, it creates them and reacts after the fact without knowing the true origin of events.

Neville's method is simplicity itself. It can be reduced to a three-step formula:

1. Form an absolutely clear sense of what you want—be starkly honest with yourself about an accomplishment, possession, or relationship that you desire with all your heart and intellect. "Feeling is the secret," Neville wrote.

2. Enter into a state of restful physical immobility, such as what you experience just before drifting off to sleep at night (this is sometimes called the hypnagogic state)—and you are free to do this step at that time. When the mind and body are blissfully relaxed, your intellect is unusually supple and suggestible.

3. From this state of physical stillness, picture a short, emotionally satisfying scene that implies the fulfillment of your desire, such as someone shaking your hand in congratulations, or feeling the weight and density of an award in your

hands or a wedding ring on your finger. Do not witness the scene as if you're passively watching it on a movie screen, but *feel yourself in it*. Run this scene through your mind for as long as it remains vivid and satisfying. You can allow yourself to fall asleep after doing this.

Neville grew up in an era when young people were expected to venture out into the world at an early age. Born in 1905 to an English family in the West Indies, the island-born teenager, hungry to experience more of life, migrated to New York City in the early 1920s, at age 17, to study theater. Neville's ambition for the stage eventually faded as he encountered various mystical and occult philosophies. By the early 1930s, Neville embarked on a new and unforeseen career as a lecturer and writer of mind-power metaphysics. In his lectures, Neville often referred to an enigmatic, turbaned black man named Abdullah, whom Neville said tutored him in Scripture, number mysticism, Kabbalah, and Hebrew.

Whatever the source of Neville's education, his outlook reflected not only the most occultic edge of positive mind, or New Thought, metaphysics, but also the philosophy's most intellectually stimulating expression. Neville expanded on the theme of how each of us is literally the Creator clothed in human flesh, slumbering to his own divinity. We live, Neville said, within an infinite network of coexistent realities, from which we select (rather than create) experiences by the nature of our emotionalized thoughts and expectations. In that sense, the words you are now encountering are your own words—they are rooted in you, as you are ultimately rooted in God. The other men and women you see about you are also branches of the Creator: We each crisscross throughout one another's universe of formative thought systems until we experience the ultimate realization—the crucifixion on the cross of awareness—that awakens us to our providential nature.

If this all seems rather breathless, let's step back for a moment. Neville was not dogmatic on any count. He defended his ideas with an elegant simplicity and merely challenged the listener: Try it. "I hope you will be bold enough to test me," he offered. Have we lost our taste for individual experimentation?

As I explore in my recent book *Magician of the Beautiful*, some of the mystic's outlook is surprisingly congruent with current concepts in quantum physics. His outlook is probably the closest mystical analog to quantum theory, with its suggestions of a subatomic particle world where objects actually react to the perspective and measurements of a conscious observer, and an infinite range of coexistent outcomes are possible.

In 1948, Neville observed: "Scientists will one day explain why there is a serial universe. But in practice, how you use this serial universe to change the future is more important."

In a modern culture rife with metaphysical voices, it may be that Neville's was not only the most radical, but also the most integral and prescient.

Neville Goddard: A Timeline

1905—Neville Lancelot Goddard is born on February 19 to a British family in St. Michael, Barbados, the fourth child in a family of nine boys and one girl.

1922—At age seventeen Neville relocates to New York City to study theater. He makes a career as an actor and dancer on stage and silent screen, landing roles on Broadway, silent film, and touring Europe as part of a dance troupe.

1923—Neville briefly marries Mildred Mary Hughes, with whom he has a son, Joseph Goddard, born the following year.

1929—Neville marked this as the year that begin his mystical journey: "Early in the morning, maybe about three-thirty or four o'clock, I was taken in spirit into the Divine Council where the gods hold converse." (lecture from *Immortal Man*)

1931—After several years of occult study, Neville meets his teacher Abdullah, a turbaned black man of Jewish descent. The pair work together for five years in New York City.

1938—Neville begins his own teaching and speaking.

1939—Neville publishes his first book, *At Your Command*.

1940–1941—Neville meets Catherine Willa Van Schumus, who is to become his second wife.

1941—Neville publishes his longer and more ambitious book, *Your Faith Is Your Fortune*.

1942—Neville marries Catherine, who later that year gives birth to their daughter Victoria. Also that year, Neville publishes *Freedom for All: A Practical Application of the Bible*.

1942–1943—From November to March, Neville serves in the military before returning home to Greenwich Village in New York City. In 1943, Neville is profiled in *The New Yorker.*

1944—Neville publishes *Feeling Is the Secret.*

1945—Neville publishes *Prayer: The Art of Believing.*

1946—Neville meets mystical philosopher Israel Regardie in New York, who profiles him in his book *The Romance of Metaphysics.* Neville also publishes his pamphlet *The Search.*

1948—Neville delivers his classic "Five Lessons" lectures in Los Angeles, which many students find the clearest and most compelling summation of his methodology. It appears posthumously as a book.

1949—Neville publishes *Out of This World: Thinking Fourth Dimensionally.*

1952—Neville publishes *The Power of Awareness.*

1954—Neville publishes *Awakened Imagination.*

1955—Neville hosts radio and television shows in Los Angeles.

1956—Neville publishes *Seedtime and Harvest: A Mystical View of the Scriptures*.

1959—Neville undergoes the mystical experience of being reborn from his own skull. Other mystical experiences follow into the following year.

1960—Neville releases a spoken-word album.

1961—Neville publishes *The Law and the Promise*; the final chapter, "The Promise," details the mystical experience he underwent in 1959, and others that followed.

1964—Neville publishes the pamphlet *He Breaks the Shell: A Lesson in Scripture*.

1966—Neville publishes his last full-length book, *Resurrection*, composed of four works from the 1940s and the contemporaneous closing title essay, which outlines the fullness of his mystical vision and of humanity's realization of its deific nature.

1972—Neville dies in West Hollywood at age 67 on October 1 from an "apparent heart attack" reports the *Los Angeles Times.* He is buried at the family plot in St. Michael, Barbados.

About the Author

A widely known voice of esoteric ideas, **Mitch Horowitz** is a writer-in-residence at the New York Public Library, lecturer-in-residence at the Philosophical Research Society in Los Angeles, and the PEN Award–winning author of books including *Occult America; One Simple Idea: How Positive Thinking Reshaped Modern Life*; and *The Miracle Club: How Thoughts Become Reality*. Mitch is the author of G&D Media's Napoleon Hill Success Course series, including *The Miracle of a Definite Chief Aim; The Power of the Master Mind*; and *Secrets of Self-Mastery*. Mitch also edits and narrates G&D's Condensed Classics series.

About Neville

Born to an English family in Barbados, **Neville Goddard** (1905–1972) moved to New York City at age seventeen to study theater. In 1932, he abandoned his work as a dancer and actor to fully devote himself to his career as a metaphysical writer and lecturer. Using the solitary pen name Neville, he became one of the twentieth century's most original and charismatic purveyors of the philosophy generally called New Thought. Neville wrote more than ten books and was a popular speaker on metaphysical themes from the late 1930s until his death. Possessed of a self-educated and eclectic intellect, Neville exerted an influence on a wide range of spiritual thinkers and writers, from Joseph Murphy to Carlos Castaneda. The impact of his ideas continues to be felt in some of today's best-selling works of practical spirituality.

Printed in the USA
CPSIA information can be obtained
at www.ICGtesting.com
JSHW012043140824
68134JS00033B/3230